Angry Black Man

OUR EYES STILL WEEP

By Kendall Thompson

KENDALL THOMPSON

Angry Black Man

Copyright © 2020 by Kendall Thompson. All rights reserved.
No part of this book may be reproduced in any form or by any electronic or mechanical means, including information storage and retrieval systems, without written permission from the author, except for the use of brief quotations in a book review.

Angry Black Man

Table of Contents

Unfinished Product 6
Spurned 7
Excuse me, I am talking! 8
Revolution 9
Shudder 10
Angry Black Man 11
Ignorante Made 12
Razed by Storms 13
Seeds of Change 14
Winds of Change 15
Tongue In Cheek 16
Toppled 17
Want More! 18
Marionette 19
Conflicted 20
Read'em and Weep 21
Viewpoints 22
We Still Weep 23
Moralless 24
Hateful 25
City Strife 26
Genuflect 27
Slurring 28
Leave 29
Amoral 30

The Mis-Story	*31*
Followed	*32*
Anxious Empathy	*33*
The Liar's Truth	*34*
Black to White	*35*
Mine Free	*36*
A Book by its Cover	*37*
Am I Welcome	*38*
A Room's View!	*39*
ACKNOWLEDGEMENT	*40*
ABOUT THE AUTHOR	*41*

Angry Black Man

For those of us who still weep!

Unfinished Product

A grape has been crushed
A wine still kept in the dark

The fermentation process incomplete
We are that unfinished product

We have not reached our full potential
We are still delicate and fresh from the vine

We were ripe to be picked and macerated
Your pigeage made us better over time

Soon the unfinished product, will mature and come of age

Swirl, smell, taste, and savor
The color depends on the berry

We are that unfinished product
A fine wine in its beginning phase

You are a rookie sommelier, who has yet to learn to savor taste!

Spurned

I pledge allegiance to a flag?
For a flag I should give my life?

I pledge allegiance to a flag?
Of me, the hatred, is rife!

The color red, hardiness and valor, white represents purity and innocence

Blue, represents vigilance, perseverance and justice

The difficult conditions that I have endured, red is the color I bleed

The white is surely not innocent and thrives off of impunity

The blue has kept us vigilant, as we try to get home at night

We persevered your injustices, and we've done so our entire lives

I pledge allegiance to a flag?
I can't get a pledge in return?

I pledge allegiance to the flag but at every juncture I have been spurned!

Angry Black Man

Excuse me, I am talking!

It is my turn to talk, I don't want you to just hear

I want for you to listen, let it sink into your ears

I can tell that you're just hearing me, listening is not being done

We are having the same conversations, since our conversations have begun

Excuse me, I am talking, you aren't listening, is my fear

I guess I will continue talking until you uncover your listening ears!

Revolution

We will start a revolution
We will take it to the streets

These are great ideas, but none are truly unique

We should start a revolution, as our parents did long ago

We should take it to the streets and implore our brothers and sisters to vote

Let us start a revolution, our power cannot be outweighed

Let us take it to the streets, don't quiver, or go astray

We will start a revolution
We will take it to the streets

When we gain a majority of the judges, we have led to their defeat!

Angry Black Man

Shudder

Listen to what I'm saying, I will let you choose how it is being said

Sit with me and have a conversation, you don't have to be afraid

I will hold a civil conversation, if civility is being employed

I will employ a different tactic, if the need, is for me to destroy

Let us have a conversation
You can choose the medium

You can listen while I calmly speak or

You can shudder when you see me come

Let us have a conversation
I will let you choose how it is being said

I will calmly explain my position and you can listen and be afraid!

Angry Black Man

I am not the angry black man
I have lived my life with whites

All hasn't been perfect
There may have been a couple of fights

I am not the killer or the thug, that you may think I might be

I am the chief executive officer or the athletes that you see

I am your next-door neighbor in your gated communities

I too, might own a car or a fancy S.U.V.

My children may go to private schools but public schools suit me fine

I don't drink the malt liquor beer
I drink fine blends of wine

I might not use the sidewalk
I sometimes run in the street

This doesn't seem to bother you when a white person is with me

I am not the angry black man that you think that I might be

I am much more angry than the ones portrayed; the ones you see on your television screen!

Ignorante Made

What we don't know did hurt us
We were allowed to see it with our own eyes

You won't know who your parents were
Of them we will teach you to despise

We don't know why they left here
Did they actually run away

Were they lynched and then murdered
Were they sold away as slaves

Did they return to find us
Did they return to shallow graves

Did they turn to rebellion
It's much better to die as brave

Did they win their freedom
Did they fight for your freedom too

We don't know for we were made ignorant
They taught us things that just weren't true!

Razed by Storms

A storm has been a brewing, it's grown and intensified

The storm began way before I was born, it may not end while I am still alive

It formed on the coast of the motherland
It gained strength as it rode the ocean's tides

We've tracked its course and clocked its force, it has since razed apartheid

A storm is in the forecast, the forecasters, seemed, again, to get it wrong

The predictions were that it would not last and the force wouldn't be this strong

The storm has made its landfall, it's razing ideologies, like racism, of course

It's razing systems of oppression; voter suppression and use of force

How are things rebuilt?
Rebuilt, after a razing by a storm?

Will there be just more of the same?
Will what was razed be forever gone?

Seeds of Change

Seeds of change have been planted

Integration and the end of Jim Crow

Seeds of change have been planted

We still have to reap what we sow

The land where the seeds are planted must be maintained

If not maintained, overrun with weeds

Change is the crop that must be cultivated

We are the farmers and we must reseed!

Winds of Change

*It is not just a little breezy
These winds are gale force winds*

They have not yet reached their highest speeds, yet, they have started to topple things

Oppression, suppression, and racism, will not survive its gusts

Winds of change are necessary, for our survival the winds are a must

*Let not apathy be our windbreaker
Let the winds blow in unabated*

The winds of change necessary, even though there are those that will hate it!

Angry Black Man

Tongue In Cheek

Is it truly possible that every time that this man speaks?
His gaffes can be explained as purely tongue in cheek?

The ears of a weary nation are eager to receive
Remarks, laden with facts and confidence but his, beleaguering

Improper medications, slow the testing down
No longer a need to quarantine, the words spewed by this clown

I am the president of law and order
I will use our military in our streets

The president is most powerful
This is this man's belief

"I will be re-elected "hear ye, hear ye, look at me"
I hope these words buffoonish and he is speaking tongue in cheek!

Angry Black Man

Toppled

Standing for many a century, showing the pride of the south

Reminders of a time, since passed, but a time, not long ago

"Plessy versus Ferguson", separate but equal, for many still feared

"Brown versus The Board of Education", was within sixty years

Slowly but surely being toppled
Though they've stood for a century or more

Your cause doesn't support our ideals

What else do we have in store

In order to provide a more perfect union

Home of the brave and the free?

Institutionalized Racism will be toppled, just you wait and see!

Angry Black Man

Want More!

You must want more for yourself than they are willing to give?

How do you beat the expectation that you don't have long to live?

You can easily get the ammo for the weapons by which you kill!

Have you ever asked yourself why?

Why can't you get housing, why can't you be gainfully employed, why can't you get an education, why healthcare, you can't afford?

Why?

Let us explore

When did you learn that you are a descendant from Kings and Queens?

When did you learn those were racist thoughts in the songs you were taught to sing?

Have you learned, to take up arms, is not the only way?
Have you learned that they pick the judges, and, in the end, they rule the day?

You must want more?
Why don't you explore?

How can you get an education even if it means you must be self-taught?
Your moral turpitude can't be bartered nor can it be bought!

You do want more!

Don't be ignored!

Marionette

I am not really a president, but I play one on T.V.
If you look more closely, you could probably see the strings

He raises his hands, my limbs will move
If my mouth moves, his voice is heard

When I perform at rallies, it becomes the theater of the disturbed

A marionette's a puppet, it's controlled by attached strings

How else can it be justified?
Why else would I do and say these things?

Angry Black Man

Conflicted

Some march for they, are allies, of those directly affected

Some march for they feel our country needs to travel in a different direction

The flashpoint, a man being throttled, a knee on his neck, till he lay dead

This left a trail of those conflicted, to serve and protect was the officer's pledge!

I can't hate the police; he is just a bad apple in a good bunch!

I guess you didn't see his comrades, you didn't want to see them, my hunch!

Is this the reason your conflicted?

He was sworn to serve and protect who?

Is this the reason you're conflicted?

Does the who, they were sworn to serve and protect, have to look like you?

Angry Black Man

Read'em and Weep

Twelve shot in the streets yesterday
Today someone shot twelve more

What about Chicago and Seattle, is this your only retort?

What about those and the others riddled with crime?

What about our government?
Criminals of a different kind!

Subversion of foreign governments, an insatiable lust for oil!

On our public city streets, troops are being deployed!

Build a wall, not just any wall, the most beautiful wall of all times!

When someone is killed by a mob of whites, you scream out, what about black on black crime?

I hesitantly read the news reports, afraid of what I might see!

Loss of life, in mass shootings, in churches, schools, and in city streets!

I can't watch the news
I refuse to read your posts

I guess I should have read'em and wept

I wake up every morning, wondering what happened while I slept?

Angry Black Man

Viewpoints

I try to see your point of view
I would like for you to see mine

You feel you're being singled out
I feel you've been purposefully blind

You want to speak of white power
Black power is a threat

You can't see one is the problem and the other a response to that?

When you feel you're ready, it may take a little more time

You will see it from my point of view
This is when you have opened your eyes!

We Still Weep

Why do our eyes still weep?
There are still many being killed!

We didn't say it would be easy, this has happened for four hundred years!

We didn't receive our reparations, so financially, we are far behind!

Some received their reparations, but they were a skin color of a different kind!

So, you see there is a head start for you but not for me!

This is, one of the reasons, why our eyes constantly weep!

Angry Black Man

Moralless

What is that you stand for? A pledging to a flag?

Would you stand on the side of right, for your fellow man?

Would you march against injustice, for the sake of generations to come?

Are you one of the moralless, who is afraid of what the world could become?

Moralless; without morals; immoral, or corrupt

If you believe that you have morals, I suggest you look it up!

How do you feel you stand for what is right, because your pocketbook is flush?

What about those in the streets, who are, begging just to have enough?

What's your definition of morals, to defend that which is wrong?

I guess you didn't look morals up?
You've been moralless all along!

__Hateful__

Where did all your hate come from?
Did you learn this from your God?

You use the word lesbian as if it was an insult
You say homosexual agenda, as if they aren't human beings

You, the hated black man, not a white man, of all things

Where does all your hate come from
I find it kind of odd

I can't believe you can call yourself a saintly man of God!

City Strife

The bullets, pesky, like so many flies on a pile of manure
Who knows what the body count will become?

Is this a battle between rival gangs
Is this the battle to be number one?

This used to be Compton, Baltimore, or New Orleans

Richmond lived at number one, New York City,
Chicago, and Washington D.C.

They give you ammunition to give them ammunition

You kill each other in the streets

The lines extend as far as the eyes can see

The mourners' line as long as those who wait to eat

City Strife is not living

Strife is not life

We must stop the killing!

Angry Black Man

Genuflect

Beaten and made to genuflect
Take a knee and you're abhorred

The sheer dichotomy, is that which, keeps us forlorn

Kneel before your master, to bring attention to a cause, genuflect

You don't mind my kneeling, unless you feel it's showing disrespect?

Take a knee for the entire world to see, is disrespectful to those who have served

I find it quite ironic; he was killed by the oppressor's knee, and some feel it well deserved

Genuflect, a gesture to show respect
Kneel to bring attention to a cause

The fact that one is believed to show disrespect, should bring us more than a momentary pause!

Slurring

What words do you use to show your hate?
To disrespect, belittle, and denigrate

Do you not, see how this equates?

A nigger, a kaffir, a jigaboo?

A bible thumper, cafeteria Christian, a hymie, a Jew boy, too?

A faggot, carpet muncher, tail gunner, a queer

Spewed in hate to offend another's ears!

You've learned to read but who created the words?

Slurs are made up and are meant to sound absurd

Slurring is not just done by the intoxicated or the sick

Maybe we have been taught to be ill, when you think of it!

(Slurring- spewing words of hate to disparage another)

Angry Black Man

<u>Leave</u>

We built this country as we shed blood
We lost our identities over the last four hundred years

You asking me to leave doesn't nearly bring me to tears

I will stay to annoy you and accentuate all of your fears

Your son will fall in love with her
Your daughter in love with me

You will be outnumbered and become the minority

The answer to your problems is not for us to simply leave

The answers to our problems is for all to be treated equally!

"If you don't like it, you should simply up
and leave"

Why should I leave a country that was built on the backs of those who looked like me?

Amoral

You're concerned about a city?
Is your concern legitimate?

You question "where is the outrage", "where is the marching, the lament?"

You don't want to control the weapons that flow freely onto the streets

Your legitimate concerns fall on deaf ears and are incomplete

You don't want to control the weaponry, the ammunition, the influx of guns

Doesn't make you wonder where these killers get all of the funds

You scream that you have morals
I scream, you have nothing of the sort

There is no way you know what morals means
Maybe the word you seek, is amoral?

The Mis-Story

Before I learned your history, I should have had the option to know of mine

Why would you change the facts, why keep me purposely blind?

Those who know their history, have a foundation on which to build

So you purposely kept the truth from me, so, it was to you, that I would yield

Proudly taught your history, just, as if, your same, was mine

Why wouldn't you expect the mis-story to be exposed, over centuries, over time?

Proudly taught the mis-story, over centuries, over time

History for you and that for me share the fact that they are intertwined!

Followed

I know that I am being followed
I am walking down my neighborhood street

I know that he is following me
He is being overtly non-discreet

Maybe he has been dispatched for a suspicious person walking near
He can't think that person is me, I have lived here for twenty-five years

I am being followed
I just walked into the store

I guess the people who used to know me, aren't working here anymore

"May I help you?" Is the greeting
Letting me know, "we have our eyes on you!"

I know I am being followed for this is just what I am used to

I know I am being followed for I can plainly see

I have to record my interactions; in case something should happen to me!

Anxious Empathy

We have empathy for your anxiety
You see we have lived your life before

You don't know what the future holds
You don't know what life has in store

What is this word posterity. In the preamble, is this word for me

What about my family's heritage. What about our history

I have a right of an existence. I can't allow a treatment less

I stand up for what I feel is right
While you fight it with zeal and zest

There has been a miseducation
These are heroes of the confederacy

There has been a miseducation
These are the United States, so they are traitors to she!

How will I tell our story
I have generations that will follow me

How did we have to find our kin
Through search and oral history

So, I understand your anxiety
My ancestors sold as slaves!

All the long being taught the words Land of the Free and Home of the Brave!

The Liar's Truth

A mouth awash with falsehoods
Speak it plain, it speaks in lies

Some are not made to tell the truth
There are many things they must hide

The lie is the liars comforter, for the bed they lay in is cold

The liar would perish rather quickly, if the liar allowed the truth to be told

If you listen closely and see the truth with your own eyes

The liar has nothing to like
The liar warrants, despise

Let the truth seeker remain vigilant
The liar has many it will please

The truth and the lie aren't far apart, just know that they've changed a few things!

Angry Black Man

Black to White

The flavor, of our cities, has changed
In the city, our people barely remain

In past times, the waterfront housed the blacks
When the water was cleaned, you know what happened after that

Gentrification, something that is real
Properties once downtrodden, now given more visual appeal

Turning a neighborhood from black to white
Done in a way that people don't even put up a fight

Taxes raised; properties bequeathed
Houses and land pulled up, like carpet, from beneath our feet

Chocolate City no longer exists
The city made better, is the prevailing myth

Over time the city will change right back
When they want the suburbs again, it will change from white to black!

Angry Black Man

Mine Free

*Many a man have lost a life
So, I could live mine free*

*I just don't speak of the great wars
For there are others important to me*

*The Malcom's, Martin's, John's and more
Also paid the price*

*Of being taken from this earth
Assassins took each life*

*They took their lives but not the dreams
They were woven in the fabric*

*The fabric of a country's quilt
That covers even the average*

*So, let us keep their dreams alive by making every effort
Of simply lending a helping hand to each and every neighbor*

Angry Black Man

A Book by its Cover

Am I purely what you see?

Surely there is more to me!

What you see by happen stance.

Cannot be known by the first glance!

To read my pages first you must earn, the chance to meet me then you will learn

There is more to me than meets the eye!

The smart, the witty and caring I!

When you first see me, you should not frown.

I'm not just a hue of tan and brown!

There is more to me than meets the eye!
Judge not a book by its cover and nor will I!

<u>Am I Welcome</u>

I give my thank you to the elders!
Who helped me to succeed?

While allowing me to be, Who I was born to be

Your birthplace is not chosen, But your friends, your schools, your hood
Are places that are chosen, But it is understood

You might encounter questions!
People will gawk and stare!

They wonder how you got the means, To end up living there
They look at what you're driving, They try to guess your pay

They hope that their young daughters, Don't bring you home one day

This is the life that's lived, By a man with a hue of brown
Do you feel that he is welcome, In the place you call your town?

A Room's View!

In a room full of people, not like me, I am not afraid!

In a room of people, not like you, would you ever stay?

Could you stand the stares, the whispers beneath the breaths?

Would you engage in conversation before you up and left?

Are you afraid in a crowd that looks like me?

Do you act most brave, in a crowd that looks like you?

Will you worry how they perceive you or can you change their point of view?

ACKNOWLEDGEMENT

A tremendous thank you goes out to my wife Kathy and our children Victoria and Kendall Jr. It isn't easy putting up with an old man. Thank you to PJ Devlin! You have delivered me to my writer's destination. Thank you to the countless unnamed people whose struggles give me thought. Thank you, Stephanie White, for reading and comparing me to some of the greats. I appreciate you all.

                On the cover: Jeffrey Thompson

ABOUT THE AUTHOR

Kendall Thompson dedicated his life to protecting his community as a Firefighter. He's a member of a proud African American family with deep roots in Alexandria, Virginia and a history of community service. Kendall is a long-distance runner and family man. His poems spring from his soul as he struggles to balance his lifetime of service with his lifetime of racial disregard. His poetry is his quiet call to action, expressing his belief in the power of shared understanding.

Angry Black Man is the author's second book of verse. He has also written WHY WE WALK IN THE STREET.

www.ingramcontent.com/pod-product-compliance
Lightning Source LLC
Chambersburg PA
CBHW031507040426

42444CB00007B/1244